I0142003

NOTES ON THE EMPLOYMENT OF WOMEN ON MUNITIONS OF WAR

WITH AN APPENDIX ON
TRAINING *of* MUNITION WORKERS

The Naval & Military Press Ltd.

Published by

The Naval & Military Press Ltd
Unit 5 Riverside, Brambleside
Bellbrook Industrial Estate
Uckfield, East Sussex
TN22 1QQ England

Tel: +44 (0)1825 749494

www.naval-military-press.com
www.nmarchive.com

*In reprinting in facsimile from the original, any imperfections are inevitably reproduced
and the quality may fall short of modern type and cartographic standards.*

CONTENTS

3

PREFACE

THIS book has been prepared by an expert engineer, who at my request visited workshops in various parts of the country where the dilution of skilled labour is in actual operation. It illustrates some of the operations which women, with the loyal co-operation and splendid assistance of the workmen concerned, are performing in engineering shops in many parts of the kingdom.

The photographic records and the written descriptions of what is actually being done by women in munition factories, on processes hitherto performed solely by skilled men, will, I believe, act as an incentive and a guide in many factories where employers and employed have been sceptical as to the possibilities of the policy of dilution.

Being convinced that until that policy is boldly adopted throughout the country we cannot provide our armies with such an adequate supply of munitions as will enable them to bring this war to an early and successful conclusion, I very earnestly commend this book to the most serious consideration of employers and employed.

The thanks of the Ministry of Munitions are due to the gentleman who prepared the book, and to the firms who granted him facilities for the photographs to be taken, or themselves supplied the negatives.

D. Lloyd George

Ministry of Munitions of War,
  6 Whitehall Gardens, S.W.
January 28th, 1916.

NOTE

THE material collected for the preparation of this book has been so abundant that the photographs included in it represent only a small portion of the operations performed by women of which detailed information with photographs is now available. These photographs have been indexed and arranged under the trade or operation which they represent; they are at the service of firms considering the dilution of labour, and can be examined at the office of the Ministry of Munitions, 6 Whitehall Gardens, London, S.W.

WOMEN ON 18-PDR. H.E. SHELLS

DRILLING OPERATIONS

WHEN the machines illustrated were first installed unskilled men (one operator per machine) were trained by a skilled driller. After a time it was found that, owing to the operation requiring seven minutes to complete, one man could easily work two machines. Twist drills were first used, but these were afterwards replaced by flat cutters made in the firm's tool room and cutter bars of nickel steel. It was then observed that by considerably increasing the flow of water, cuttings were more readily washed out of the bore and the machines did not require such close attention.

After a few weeks the firm started a new shop for machining a heavier size of shell, and the drilling machine operators, who had previously been entirely unskilled, were now deemed sufficiently good to draft into a new and larger shop as shell turners on engine lathes. Women had previously been working on simple lathe operations in the shop where the 18-pounder drilling machines are installed, and a number were then drafted on to the drilling machines to replace the men transferred to the 6-in. Shell Shop.

The output of these drilling machines has been maintained under the new conditions, and the women complain of no fatigue or difficulty whatever in carrying out this operation. It is advisable to provide them with waterproof aprons, and to arrange that between each machine is a raised wooden platform, so that both the feet and dress of the operator are kept dry.

Only one change has been made in the machines to suit the women. At first the shell blanks were dropped into a round jig, and owing to the speed of drilling the blank was frequently wedged in the chuck after the drilling was completed. To avoid the heavy work of forcing the shell out of the chuck, a new type, designed by the drilling machine maker, was fitted ; this is clearly shown in the small photograph on the following page. The depth of the hole is regulated by an automatic cut-off.

One male supervisor (an unskilled workman) is provided for each eight machines, and the blanks are brought up to the machines in trucks designed for the purpose.

DRILLING 18-pdr. SHELL BLANKS

ONE woman is operating *two* drilling machines. The time of operation is seven minutes, and this interval allows the finished work to be removed and the new blank chucked without fatigue to the operator. Inset is the chuck, showing the simple manner in which the work is held and changed on completion of operation.

WOMEN ON 18-PDR. AND 4·5 H.E. SHELLS

ENGINE LATHE OPERATIONS

THE operations of rough turning and finishing the profile together with the boring of the cavity have now been carried out by women in all parts of the country and with complete success. The number of wasters produced has been materially reduced by sub-dividing each complicated operation into a number of simple ones. Further, the addition of stops which prevent the tool turning below a certain size and also automatic cut-off devices on boring lathes have still further decreased the chance of spoiled work. In the roughing operations the women have proved to be capable of operating *not only one lathe, but two.* It has been found that, owing to several minutes being occupied whilst the tool is traversing across the face of the shell, it is easily possible to remove the finished blank from the other lathe and replace it by another, ready for machining, without any loss of output due to this duplication of work.

It is not suggested that women be asked to operate two machines as a general rule. The sole object of this and the foregoing example is to show that, if one woman can continuously operate two machines, the handling of one machine is, without doubt, a perfectly simple achievement.

To the left, in the upper illustration on page 10, women are operating two machines each on 18-pounder shell bodies. These particular tools are fitted with a type of tool-post which enables a spare tool to be carried, so that, in the event of one failing, the other can be quickly brought into operation without stoppage of output. The automatic stops fitted to the lathes give the women confidence that they can proceed with the work boldly without spoiling the shell.

The lower illustration gives a general view of a shop carrying out all the operations, up to band turning, on 4·5 H.E. shells.

In this particular factory there are three shifts per day of 24 hours, with two breaks for meals and an additional break of ten minutes in the middle of the long shift.

Time-keeping in the factories employing women on projectile work is excellent, *the record being so good as to make it difficult to express lost time as a percentage.*

9

SECTION I.—SHELL BODIES—*continued*

It will be noticed that one woman is working *two* engine lathes.

General view of 4·5 Shell Gallery :
It has been found that up to 4·5 shell, lifting appliances are unnecessary,
and all the illustrations are taken from factories in which hand-lifting is
employed on shells up to the size mentioned.

SMALL DETAIL OPERATIONS

WHERE operations are short and women are constantly changing the work in Collet chucks minor alterations to the gear are advisable to decrease physical strain. Inset is a draw-in device designed to give considerable leverage with a small effort on the part of the operator. It has been found that on both night and day shifts the operators are able to keep the lathes running constantly without fatigue. Several installations of plant have now been operated day and night for six months, without appreciable strain on the women employed. Certain delicate operations, such as turning the copper band, were originally done by men, but many employers now find that if special fittings are designed, such as those shown on pages 12 and 14, women carry out the work with complete satisfaction.

Inset on next page will be noticed a photograph giving greater detail of the copper band-turning device. The limit of accuracy called for on delicate operations like the driving band was such as to encourage amongst employers the view that the number of bands spoiled by women workers would more than neutralise the saving to the country by the employment of this type of labour. The illustration shows the precautions adopted for preventing bands being turned either too small in diameter or incorrect in form. (See also page 14.)

One male setter-up maintains in constant operation nine band-turning lathes. The operations carried out on the group of lathes illustrated comprise: Ending off to weight ; taking out the base ; gashing and undercutting and waving for the band groove ; finish band-turning.

Inspection of the finished shell is, subject to sufficient specialisation being employed, a class of work in which women have been very successful.

In the case illustrated each woman has been trained to the use of one or two gauges only, and this ultra-specialisation has resulted in an efficiency such as cannot generally be obtained by a highly skilled male inspector using a large number of gauges. Women have achieved extraordinary proficiency in detecting loose base plugs or loose copper bands at the inspection bench.

General view of 18·pdr. shop entirely operated by women.

DETAIL OPERATIONS SUBSEQUENT TO BORING

One operator per machine, lathes similar in type but set up for eight different operations. Machines on left of picture turning copper bands, those on right gashing and undercutting body for banding groove.

12

SECTION 1.—SHELL BODIES—*continued*

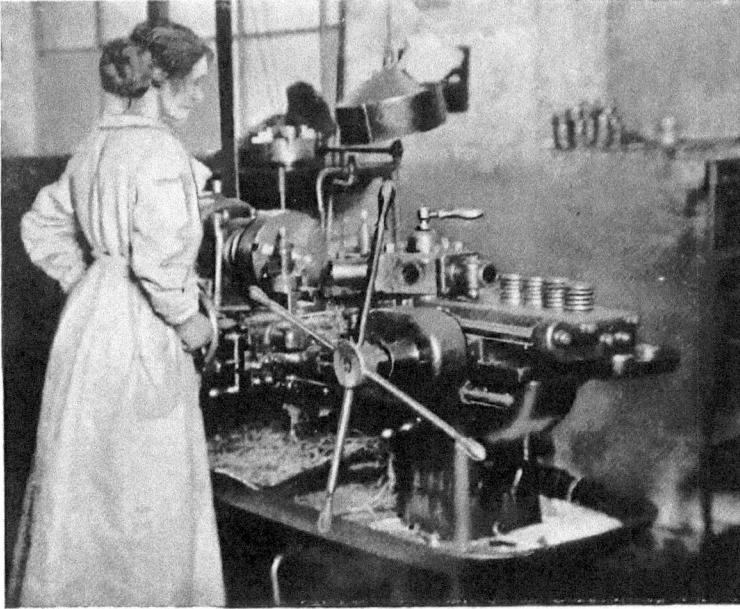

Turning base plates for shells on turret lathe.

Cutting copper bands for shells from tubes.

Pressing on copper bands.

Turning copper bands on high explosive shell. Tool-holders specially designed to prevent band being turned incorrectly.

Riveting Base Plug on H.E. Shell Bodies. This operation is quite suitable for women, and if the jigs are properly designed to facilitate changing the work, practically continuous operation can be secured.

Detail of jig for holding shell.

Ripping nose of 4'5 shell forging to length before rough turning.

Group of lathes roughing and finishing the bore on 4'5 shell.

6-IN. AND 8-IN. SHELL BODIES

THERE has been, and is still, some difference of opinion amongst engineers as to the employment of women on shells of 6-inch calibre and upwards, and the following illustrations are taken from factories actually and continuously employing female labour on these heavier shells. The experience of those employing woman labour on large shell bodies is that the actual cutting operations demand no greater strain from the operator than do those on smaller shell, but that the lifting in and out is the all-important factor in the operations on heavy shell.

Owing to the fact that women have only recently been employed on the heavier shells some factories are using, temporarily, lifting devices which are obviously capable of considerable improvement. Illustrated is a case where an ordinary block swung on a small jib attached to the lathe is proving quite satisfactory. It is obvious, however, that fairly elaborate lifting appliances are essential for efficient operation, and constitute a deciding factor in the employment of women on heavy projectiles.

Some of the newer factories not yet in full operation are using special bogies embodying lifting appliances which render the handling of shells of large calibre a matter requiring no physical strain whatever. Given, therefore, satisfactory handling devices, there appears to be no reason whatever why women should not be quite as generally employed on heavy shells as on projectiles of smaller diameter.

6-in. SHELL BODIES

I T will be noticed that the lathe is of a very heavy type capable of dealing with heavy cuts. At the back of the slide, and not shown in the photograph, is a stop which prevents the tool making the shell of too small a diameter, whilst the four tool-post fitted on to the machine allows a spare tool to be carried which can be set up by gauge to the correct position, and which is ready for instant operation. Where a woman operates a tool of this size and importance, it is imperative that every precaution be taken to ensure continuous running.

6-IN. SHELL BODIES

It is advisable to design specially the apparatus for boring 6-in. shell by woman labour, so as to prevent undue breakage of cutters when the bar reaches the base of the shell. The operations illustrated show :—

The cutter rough boring the shell down the straight part before the radius is encountered ; the traverse of the bar being then automatically cut off.

The next operation shown, that of bottoming, is traversed by hand and with the aid of the lever shown in the illustration.

The third illustration shows an operator using the high and low limit gauges.

8-IN. H.E. SHELL BODIES

Illustrated are the operations of rough turning, gauging and parting-off the bodies for 8-in. H.E. shell.

On account of the great cost of the forging of a shell of this calibre, special precautions are taken to prevent any possibility of defective work, and "stops" of special construction are fitted to the slide rests; the male supervision also is slightly increased.

The lathes illustrated are supervised by one male shell turner to each four machines.

WOMEN IN GENERAL MACHINE SHOPS

T HE question of the dilution of skilled male labour by women in general munition shops is admittedly a more difficult problem than that dealt with in the previous section. In projectile work and other operations in which the pieces are manufactured in tens of thousands, and for which entirely special lathes and machines are designed, super-specialisation and sub-division of operations render women's work comparatively easy to organise. In the general machine shop, however, where pieces of work are dealt with in numbers of ten and twenty, no such special "fool-proof" devices or limitation of the number of operations per machine can be organised.

In the following pages photographs are shown in which women are operating ordinary commercial machines without special rigs on general work. The great variety of work now being carried out by women in general shops makes it impossible to show instances sufficiently comprehensive in character to cover more than the very fringe of the subject. It was therefore considered most satisfactory to take one shop and one trade, covering this with a series of photographs and examples, and then follow with a number of instances in other classes of manufacture, the latter being arranged under " types of tool." (See p. 3.)

The shop selected is a general engineering factory employing about 400 hands. The manufactures are so general as to range over locomotives, gun mountings, turret lathes and other types of machine tool. A fair amount of tool-room work is carried out, the majority of the product being sold by the firm and not used in their own factory.

The first three photographs show the method adopted by the firm for dealing with operations in which the job was obviously far too difficult for a woman without very complete and continual supervision. The method, after a prolonged trial, has proved to be an entirely satisfactory solution of a problem which will confront every shop employed on general work. It is therefore instructive to indicate in detail the system as regards payment of employees in this case.

In the first photograph are two ordinary chucking lathes. Before the introduction of women a skilled man operated each machine. The work in progress is a lathe saddle and turret, and the woman is boring the turret, which is eventually fitted to the saddle shown in the lathe on the left of the photograph. The male operator is responsible for both machines, *and the total price paid for the product of the two lathes is the same as was originally paid when two men worked these two machines.* The man gives the woman every possible assistance, and, when the total earnings of the two machines are distributed, the division is such as considerably to increase the normal earnings of the male worker. It cannot be too strongly emphasised that the amount paid for the work is not reduced in any way, so that the conditions laid down by the Ministry of Munitions with regard to the employment of women on work previously carried out by men are strictly adhered to.

Working small bar lathes on repetition work.

Operating shaping machines on tool-making work. It will be noticed that the operator in the foreground is working with a dividing head. The accurate angles required make the job a remarkable example of the accuracy of women's work.

Grinding to size and using micrometer on hardened and ground pins for registering lathe turrets. One quarter to half of one-thousandth error is sufficient to scrap the work.

Operating drilling machines on the same plan as that previously described.

Drilling holes $\frac{2}{16}$ths inches diameter. 8 inches long, in nickel chrome steel gun-carriage mountings.

24

Twelve - inch stroke slotting machines making cutter bars for turret lathes.

Special slot miller on shell-boring cutters.

Operating ordinary turret
lathes on small machine
parts. The woman ope-
rating the centre lathe
sets up her own cutters
without supervision.

Fifteen-inch centre chucking
lathe turning pulleys.

Each operator is working two milling machines. The output of the machines has been maintained at its old figure, and the quality of the work is thoroughly good.

SECTION 3.—PLANING AND SHAPING

Operating 24-in. shaping machine on machine tool parts.

Light planer on general work.

SECTION 3.—GRINDING

Grinding shafts after
rough turning.

Small grinder on
machine tool details.

Grinding faces
of lock nuts.

Operating plain
cylindrical grinder.

Grinding taper pins
for shell lathes.

Internal grinding
on friction rings.

Grinding machines on twist drill work and also internal grinding.

Grinding operation on valve-seating cutter.

SECTION 3.—GRINDING— *continued*

Gang of special grinders
on ball bearings.

Detail view of
machines.

Small surface grinder.

Gang of surface grinders on left ; on right, tap sharpening.

34

SECTION 3.—GRINDING—*continued*

Grinding friction
rings.

Grinding milling
machine cutters.

SECTION 3.—CENTRE LATHES

Rough turning preparatory to grinding.

Boring hole in lathe spindles.

Facing shafts to
length.

General turning
work.

On the left, turning cast-iron sleeves. On the right, turning shafts.

Pulley turning.

SECTION 3.—SEMI-AUTOMATIC TURRET LATHES

Gang of capstan
lathes on machine
tool parts.

Turning and boring
wheel blanks.

Gang of capstan lathes on chucking work.

Turning and boring wheel blanks.

Turning pulleys for machine tools.

Semi-automatic turret lathe set up to "stops" and on repetition work.

Turning "former" handles for machine tools.

Boring on chucking lathe with special fixture for repetition work.

Operations on self-opening die head parts. Highly accurate interchangeable work.

Machining forged steel blanks.

Semi-automatic bar lathe on small shafts.

44

SECTION 3.—HORIZONTAL MILLING MACHINES

Milling square turrets for lathes.

Milling lathe brasses shown in front of picture.

Making milling cutters. The woman is operating a horizontal milling machine on the manufacture of milling cutters. It will be noticed that the work is of the most delicate description and that a dividing head is in use on the machine. The material worked upon is high speed steel, and the number of wasters made by the operator is practically negligible.

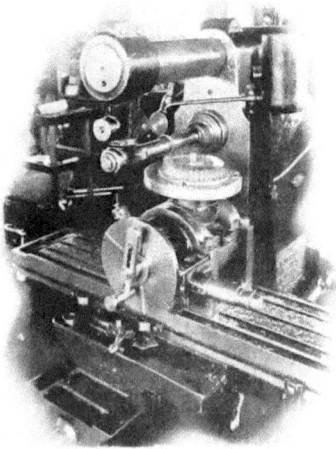

Detail of operation.

SECTION 3.—MILLING MACHINES

Milling teeth of bevel pinion, and using special dividing head and jig for taper work.

Vertical milling machine making spiral scrolls.

Slot milling machine
on machine tool parts.

Continuous milling on pump
covers. Note the simple
nature of the jig, which allows
of continuous milling. The
finished work can be removed
and new pieces put into the
jig without stopping the
machine.

SECTION 3.—KEY-WAYING MACHINES—*continued*

Slot milling for key seating.

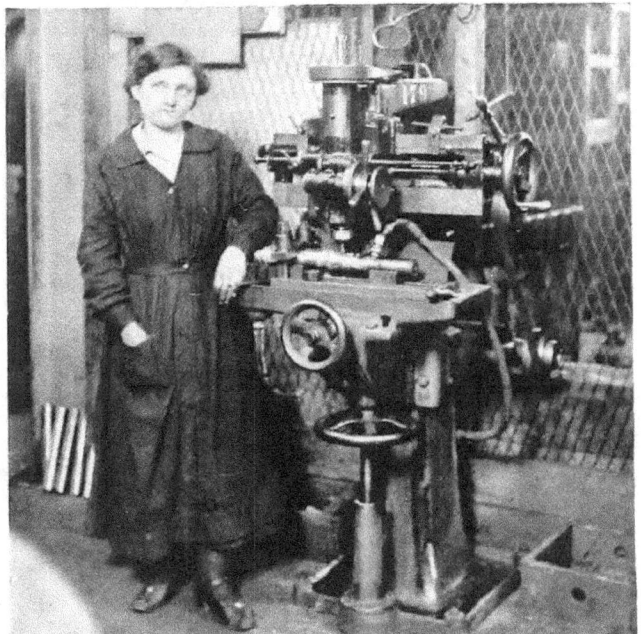

Milling key seating in shafts.

SECTION 3.—DRILLING MACHINES

Operating drilling machine on general non-repetition work.

Drilling on cast iron brackets for machine tools.

General view.
On right: gang of
light drills.
On left: assembling
cages for ball
bearings.

Detail view of
drilling operations.

SECTION 3.—DRILLING MACHINES—*continued*

Drilling small parts with multiple spindle drill.

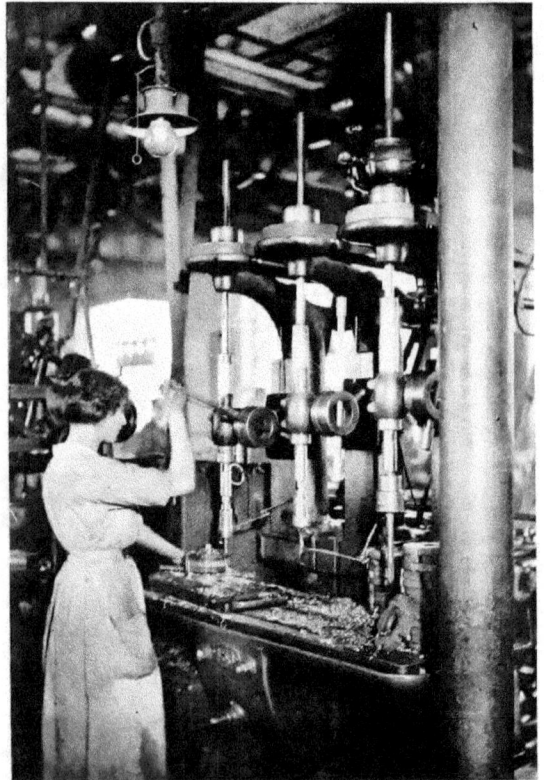

Repetition drilling on multiple spindle machine.

SECTION 3.—MISCELLANEOUS OPERATIONS

Front row : Group of backing-off lathes producing form cutters.

Back row : Double angle cutters

Detail of operation on double angle cutters.

Gear shapers.

Cutting key ways on
slotting machine.

Milling face and side of slide rest.

Shaping poppet base.

General Views in Ball Bearing Factory.

SECTION 3.—FITTING AND BENCH WORK

Fitting under supervision of male worker.

Marking off.

Fitting for machine tools.

SECTION 3.—FITTING AND BENCH WORK—*continued*

Filing up wheel blanks after machining, and preparatory
to hardening.

59

SECTION 3.—AIRCRAFT, BRAZING, WELDING, etc.

Building turbine motors.

Detail of above.

Illustrated is a department in which women are engaged on the work of assembling turbine rotors. The operations are as follows :—

(1) Preparing segment for blades.
(2) Threading blades and caulking up.
(3) Wiring up before brazing.
(4) Brazing.

Women use length gauges, true up the blades, and braze successfully without burning the blades.

Women acetylene welding.

The success of this operation is largely dependent upon the provision of face and head guards in order to minimise the onerous conditions of this class of work.

Acetylene welding.

SECTION 3.—AIRCRAFT, BRAZING, WELDING, etc.—*contd.*

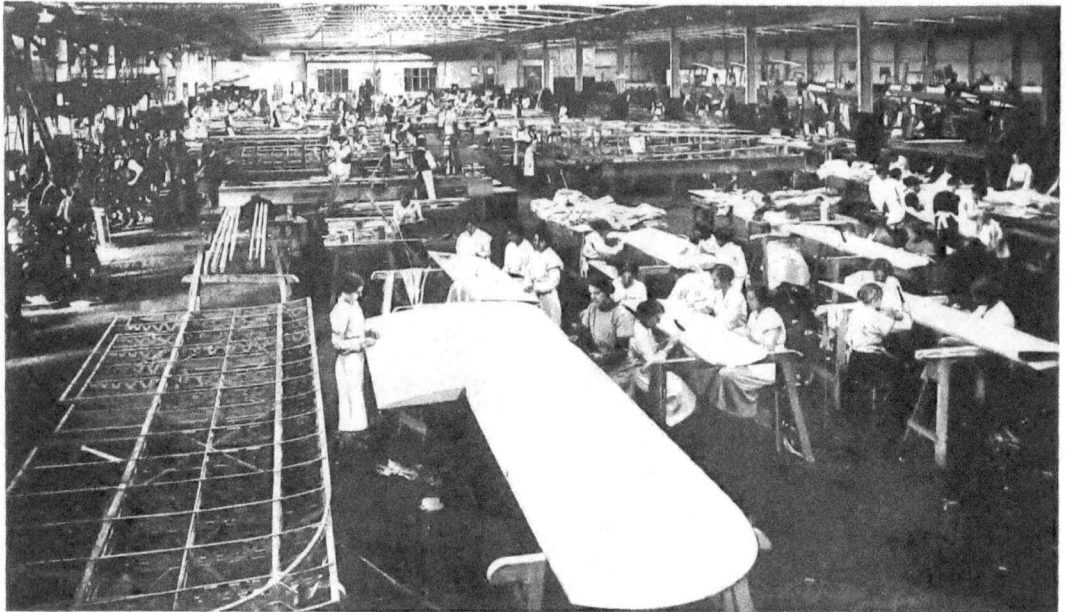

Covering aircraft wings.

General view of aircraft shop showing, on the left, women making small metal clips and fittings.   On the right, soldering flexible wires for aeroplanes.

SECTION 4.—SHELL FUSES

THE following photographs are taken from two or three typical factories, and are indicative of the entire suitability of this class of work for woman labour. The majority of successful fuse-making factories are, as regards the operation of machinery, manned entirely by women. The object of publishing these photographs is to show the grouping of machines and the scheme of general organisation employed. Organisation is a determining factor as regards output in any fuse-making factory, for the operations are so small and their number is so large as to make the handling between machines extremely important. In factories turning shell bodies, and larger pieces, the handling is a factor of great moment ; but in fuse-making factories it becomes a point, together with that of inspection, of no less importance than the bare machining time as regards quantity and quality of work.

General view of 65a Department. (Inset) Inspecting and gauging body of No. 65a Fuse.

Assembling No. 100 Fuse. (Inset) Inspecting and gauging body of No. 100 Fuse.

Tapping fuse parts.

General view of drilling
machines in main shop.
(No. 100 Fuse.)

Girl operating duplex drilling
machine on safety pin-holes
on No. 65a Fuse.

SECTION 4.—SHELL FUSES—*continued*

Trained capstan setter in charge of group of capstans operated by girls. (No. 100 Fuse.)

Man being trained as setter on fuse work.

SECTION 4.—SHELL FUSES—*continued*

View of capstan lathes on
body of No. 100 Fuse.

Detail of above.

Bottom Inset.—Detail of operation as in large photo.

Top Inset.—View of operator milling powder groove in time ring.

Group of automatic milling machines on teeth and pellet-holes on time rings.   (No. 121 Fuse.)

General view of capstan lathes on body of No. 121 Fuse.

General view of milling machines on bayonet slots for body and safety cap. (No. 44 & 18 Fuse.)

General view of drilling and assembling operation.

Spinning machine— operator adjusting and testing the shutter of No. 44 Fuse.

Girl drilling safety pin-hole —
hole breaking in and out of
three different parts. (No.
44 & 18 Fuse.)

Girl operator reducing thickness
of diaphragm to '003" and gauging
same by special micrometer.
(No. 44 & 18 Fuse.)

Assembling hand grenades and small detail parts in ammunition factory.

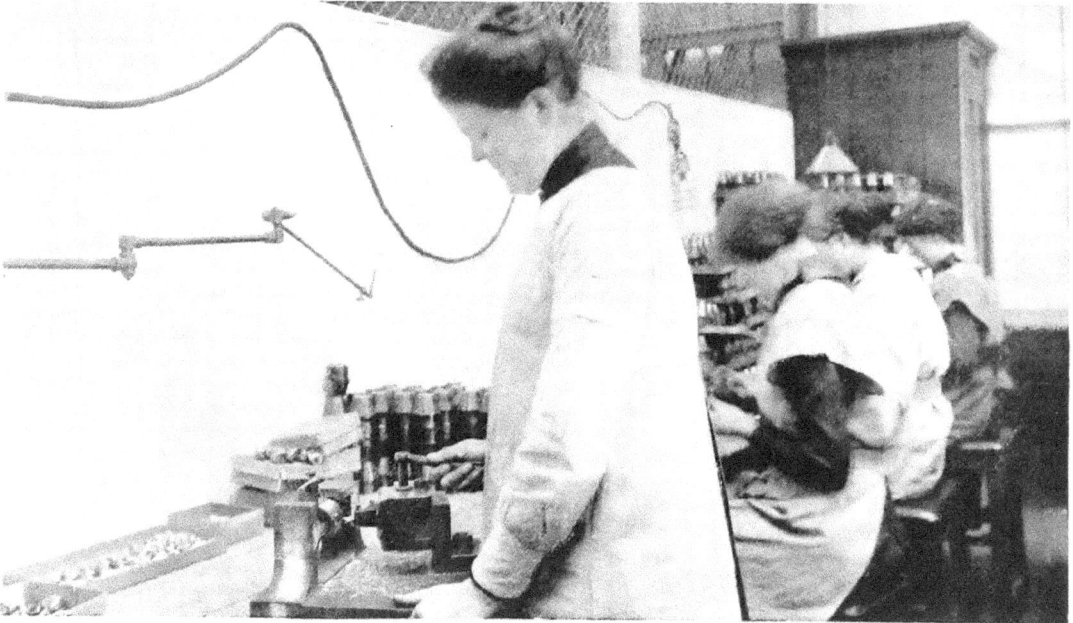

Detail operations on shell fuses.

Sundry operations on shell fuses.

APPENDIX
TRAINING OF MUNITION WORKERS

WHEN the magnitude of the Munitions Problem became apparent, it was at once obvious that every possible source of labour must be tapped. Thousands of men of superior education and intelligence were eager to assist in Munition Factories for the period of the war. These men, however, could only be efficiently employed after some preliminary training in the use of tools, and it was with a view of making available labour of this type that the Ministry of Munitions, in co-operation with the Board of Education, arranged to use the resources of Technical Schools for the training of munition workers. As, however, the men in question could only be used during the period of the war and would afterwards return to their regular occupations, the aim of the Ministry was to give only a slight knowledge of machine tools and wherever possible to confine the training to a particular operation. These men and also women were for the most part *not engaged in actual production* when they began their course. Hence every one of them is a new recruit to munition work and their employment involves no economic dislocation, such as inevitably results from the withdrawal of workers already engaged in other forms of production. Every hand taken from the woollen mills, for example, involves an economic loss ; every unemployed architect trained as a munition worker is an economic gain. It is not claimed that every one of these trained workers—and there are over 10,000 of them— has been a success, still on the whole the scheme is justified by its results. It has brought into the

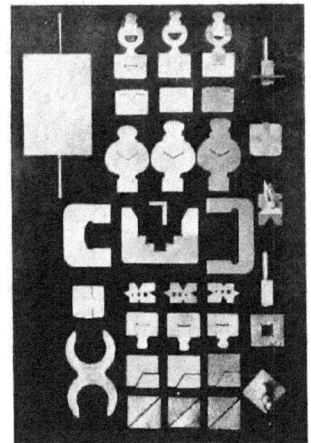

School Workshop:
Fitting and gauge - making exercises, illustrating the course of training given to students who show special aptitude for this work.

View of Workshop in
Training School.

shops thousands of workers who would not otherwise have been available, and the reports received from employers who have made a trial of these trained workers speak for the most part very favourably of their zeal and capacity.

Considerable success has been achieved in the direction of training men for the actual operation they will be called upon to perform in the factory. If an employer with an extension of his works, or a delivery of new machines in view, would indicate to the Ministry his actual needs *in advance*, specifying quite definitely the operation for which he requires the men, the training centres could deal with the matter in a thoroughly efficient manner. Some of the more progressive employers are actually doing this, and even lending the Schools typical machines to enable them to give specialised training. Although the majority of the trained operators are merely semi-skilled workers suited to repetition work in Shell Factories, it was inevitable that in so large a number there should be a fair percentage capable

School Workshop: General View.

of being trained to a much higher degree of skill. Wherever the equipment of the Technical Schools made it possible, great care has been taken to give every encouragement to those who showed real mechanical aptitude. In view of the admitted shortage of skilled workers it cannot be too strongly emphasised that, with the co-operation of employers, men and women can quickly be trained to certain limited but nevertheless skilled operations. This principle is being carried out in the schools, and pupils are expressly trained for the

School Workshop :
General view of lathes.

work on the specific machine they will eventually have to operate.

The shortage of tool setters has led to a further development. The installation of new machinery in certain schools has made it possible to train there a number of specialised tool setters that is, men who are competent to set up one particular type of machine. These tool setters on automatic and semi-automatic machines are for the most part from

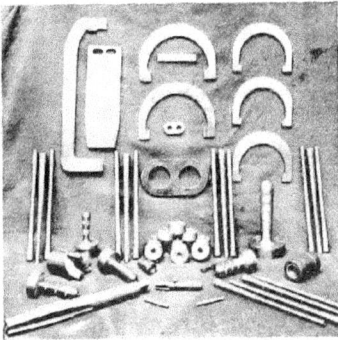

School Workshop :
Production work supplied to firms.
Gauges and tools.

the professional classes, who will naturally revert to their former avocation after the war. The necessity for employing women in greater numbers in Munition work has led to a large increase in the number of women passing through the schools. Some of the centres now train women only. The Ministry is anxious to apply and extend the methods indicated above to the training of women and to teach them in the schools the actual type of repetition work for which they will be required.   It is hoped that by the publication of this series of photographs, showing the actual operations on which these trained workers are engaged, the possibility of making a more extensive use of this scheme will be at once apparent.

Boy operating semi-automatic turret lathe on small projectile parts.

(Inset are details showing the operation at each position of the turret.)

School Workshop :
Training for special skilled operations in Ammunition Factory. Boring Bullet Dies.
Age of operator : 36 (twice rejected as medically unfit). Former occupation : Laundry work.

Detailed view of above, showing tool and reamer in position. These dies are turned, drilled and bored, and then finished with a taper reamer.

Eight men from this school have already been supplied to one firm for this special operation.

School Workshop: Shaping, milling machines, &c. (Morning Class).

School Workshop: Some of the lathes (Afternoon Class).

School Workshop: Training for special skilled operations in Ammunition Works.
Turning Cartridge Heading Pegs.
Age of operator: 38 (physically unfit for Army).   Former occupation: Grocer.

Detailed view of above, showing tools in position : Turned externally to three diameters, and bored up the centre for the anvil. Turned to micrometer to fit high and low gauges.

School Workshop: Training for special skilled operations in Ammunition Works.
Turning and Boring Cartridge Heading Dies.
Age of operator: 42.   Former occupation: Carpenter.

Detailed view of above.   These dies are turned externally to gauge ; drilled and reamered out to gauge ; and then recessed in front for the "bumper" through which the heading peg is fixed.   The view shows the reamer in position.

Detailed view of milling the tongue of 6-in. shell gauge to fit the groove for driving band.

School Workshop:
Milling 6-in. shell gauge.
Age of operator: 51.
Former occupation: Retired.

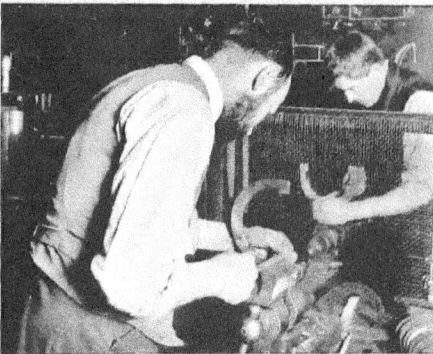

Gauge Making:
Six-inch shell horseshoe gauge.
These are finished from the blank,
leaving ten-thousandths for
grinding.
(Note.—146 of these have been made in the classes.)
Age of operator: 45.
Former occupation: Decorator.

Turning reamer for 3-pounder
H.E. shell. Also showing
finished reamer.

Trained Men in Factories.
View showing trained men in Meter Works on shell work.

Trained man engaged in turning shell adapters.
Age of operator : 35 (physically unfit for Army).
Former occupation: Architect.

Detailed view of adapter after turning, showing the various gauges used.

These adapters are brought from a capstan lathe, externally rough-turned to size, and faced to correct length. They are afterwards screwed by a chaser, working from a screwed mandril.

This operator, after a fortnight in the works, was able to turn and screw four dozen of these in nine hours.

Detailed view of same adapter being screwed.

School Workshop : Turning cartridge heading punches.
Age of operator : 61.   Former occupation : Boot Dealer.

Detailed view of turning, facing and boring cartridge case dies.

Three men have been supplied from this school to a large ammunition works after training for this operation.

Men in Factories after training, working on lathes.

School Workshop:
View of hearth, showing man hardening
his own tool.

School Workshop:
Tool-making (Filing reamer).
Age of operator : 40.
Former occupation : Builder's foreman.

Specially trained men in Cartridge Factories. Men at Fitting Bench.
Operators' ages : 37 (medical reject) and 60
Former occupations : None ,, Wood engraver.

Detailed view illustrating class of work on which the men shown above are engaged.

Specially trained men in Ammunition Factories. View of work on turret lathe, showing tools in position.

View of turret lathe (front), showing finished dies.

Detailed view of turret lathe making heading dies, showing tools in position.

Detailed view of face milling cutter also made by this Lithographic Artist

Trained men in Factories.
Man at work at fitting bench.
Age : 57.
Former occupation :
Lithographic Artist.

Detailed view of above, showing group of gauges made by above worker.

Testing the Tensile Breaking Strain of Shell Steel.

The selection of the pieces for testing is made by the Government Inspector. After the test pieces are numbered and scheduled, they are delivered to the Training Centre, where they are turned and screwed by the munition workers in training. The whole work is carried out by the students, from drilling the centres to lapping the bodies.

The upper illustration shows the initial turning operation, roughing down the body of triangular section.

The lower one shows the finished turning operation.

Drilling Hand Grenades in the Factory after training.

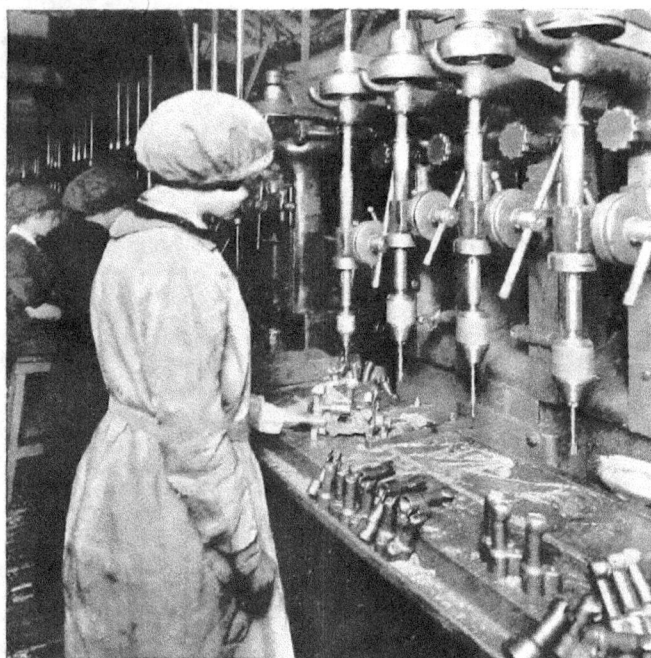

Drilling Stokes' Fuses in the Factory.

Girls at work in the Tool Room in the Factory.

Milling in the Tool Room in the Factory after a special course of training.

Turret lathe work on Stokes' Fuses in the Factory.

Turret lathe work on Hand Grenades in the Factory.

THE OFFICIAL HISTORY OF THE MINISTRY OF MUNITIONS
Compiled by HMSO - Published by The Naval & Military Press

The Official History of

THE MINISTRY
OF MUNITIONS

IMPERIAL WAR
MUSEUM

VOLUME I
INDUSTRIAL MOBILISATION
1914–15

Naval & Military Press in association with The Imperial War Museum

VOLUME I:	**Industrial Mobilizations, 1914-15** 9781847348753
VOLUME II:	**General Organization for Munitions Supply** 9781847348760
VOLUME III:	**Finance and Contracts** 9781847348777
VOLUME IV:	**The Supply and Control of Labour 1915-1916** 9781847348784
VOLUME V:	**Wages and Welfare** 9781847348791
VOLUME VI:	**Manpower and Dilution** 9781847348807
VOLUME VII:	**The Control of Materials** 9781847348814
VOLUME VIII:	**Control of Industrial Capacity and Equipment** 9781847348821
VOLUME IX:	**Review of Munitions Supply** 9781847348838
VOLUME X:	**The Supply of Munitions** 9781847348845
VOLUME XI:	**The Supply of Munitions** 9781847348852
VOLUME XII:	**The Supply of Munitions** 9781847348869

THE OFFICIAL HISTORY OF THE MINISTRY OF MUNITIONS
Compiled by HMSO - Published by The Naval & Military Press

The foundation of the Munitions Ministry was a revolutionary step, coinciding with the 'shells scandal' in which the failure of a series of British attacks: Neuve Chapelle, Aubers Ridge, Festubert and Loos – was blamed on inadequate supplies of munitions. A press outcry was followed by questions in Parliament which threatened to bring down the Government. The Ministry was set up in response. Previously, the War Office had been responsible for designing, ordering and inspecting ammunition factories and stores. But a year of war on a scale never foreseen, the creation of armies larger than ever contemplated, and the demand for unprecedented quantities of matériel showed the absolute necessity of providing centralised direction of mass war production. The Great War completely upset normal industrial conditions. Preparing this history of the Ministry of Munitions was started during the War itself. It was felt that consulting the officials concerned whilst they were still in post was vital, particularly as many such posts were temporary, and while the questions with which the history would deal were vividly present in their minds.

THE NAVAL & MILITARY PRESS
Specialist Books For The Serious Student Of Conflict

Military book enthusiasts now have a place on the internet dedicated to themselves. Our site is the most extensive devoted to military history on the web. You can browse and shop through our vast range of titles by time period or by theme, or use our advanced search facilities to find areas of specific interest.

The Naval & Military Press Ltd was founded in 1991 and quickly established itself as a mecca for the military enthusiast. Over 35,000 customers worldwide enjoy receiving our booklist which contains many hundreds of first-class books. With the advances in technology we are now pleased to show all of you with access to the internet our full catalogue. Updated regularly, you can count on the same level of service that our existing customers enjoy.

Our own publications feature strongly on both our list and our website. The innovative approach we have to military bookselling and our commitment to publishing have made us Britain's leading independent military bookseller.

Many titles featured on this website are not unavailable through any other source in the world.

www.naval-military-press.com

General Sir Ian Hamilton's
Staff Officer's Scrap-Book during the Russo–Japanese War
1904–1905
9781474538077

As Hamilton was the military attaché of the British Indian Army serving with the Japanese army in Manchuria during the Russo-Japanese War, he was well placed to publish in 1907 this impressive eye witness account to a military confrontation between a well-known European army and a less-familiar Asian army. Good maps (many in colour), a full index and 600+ pages make this facsimile two-volume set a fine reference for the modern scholar, of a war that is still the classic example of a conflict waged for purely imperialistic motives, a rivalry for the control of Korea and Manchuria and indeed for the mastery of the Far East and China.

The Golden Chersonese and the way thither
9781905748198

A delightful description of her travels in Malaya and China in the 1880s by that intrepid lady Isabella L. Bird, first female member of the Royal Geographical Society and doyenne of all women travel writers.

NOTES FROM A JOURNAL OF RESEARCH INTO THE NATURAL HISTORY OF THE COUNTRIES VISITED DURING THE VOYAGE OF H.M.S. SAMARANG under the command of Captain Sir Edward Belcher, C.B., F.R.A.S.
9781905748013

Like Darwin on the Beagle, surgeon Arthur Adams was a naturalist with this 1843-45 Naval expedition to Japan and the Indian and China Seas. Contains fascinating descriptions of the region's flora and fauna.

LOW`S HISTORY of the INDIAN NAVY
9781474536530

This is an extremely rare work, in its original edition, and covers the life span of the Indian Navy, 1600 to 1863. Operations from the Persian Gulf to the Burma and First China Wars, from Aden to New Zealand and the Maori Wars, and the Indian Mutiny. Survey work from the Red Sea to the China Seas.

NARRATIVE OF THE EARL OF ELGIN'S MISSION TO CHINA AND JAPAN IN THE YEARS 1857, '58, '59
9781905748051

Superbly illustrated two-volume account of Lord Elgin's expeditions to the Far East in 1857-59 which resulted in the occupation of Canton, the burning of Peking's Imperial Summer Palace; and the opening of Japan to European trade.

"CHINA JIM" Being Incidents and Adventures in the Life of an Indian Mutiny Veteran
9781845748463

An account of the author's experiences in the Indian Mutiny and the Second China War. The author acquired his nickname as a result of the immense amount of loot he acquired from the Summer Palace at Peking!

CHINESE WAR, AN ACCOUNT OF ALL THE OPERATIONS OF THE BRITISH FORCES 1842
9781843428176
Detailed account of the first Chinese 'Opium war' with Britain. With 53 fascinating illustrations.

VOYAGE OF HIS MAJESTY'S SHIP ALCESTE, to China, Corea, and the Island of Lewchew, with an account of her shipwreck
9781905748068
Rather aptly summed up by the title, this book was written by the ship's surgeon on the 'Alceste' which was charged with delivering the British Embassy of Lord Amherst to China in 1816. Passing through Rio de Janeiro, the Cape of Good Hope and Batavia en-route, they arrived in the China Sea in the summer and their first meetings with the Chinese together with some of the politics of the time are described here.

OFFICIAL ACCOUNT OF THE MILITARY OPERATIONS IN CHINA 1900-1901
9781783311156
This official account of the military operations in China at the time of the Boxer Rebellion and the siege of the Foreign Legations in Peking was originally compiled by Major Norrie, a member of the Intelligence Staff of the British Contingent, China Field Force. It was considerably revised, edited and expanded by the Intelligence Department at the War Office. It begins with the rise of the Boxer Secret Society and the outbreak of hostilities against foreigners in the northern provinces, extends to cover the operations for the relief of Foreign Legations in Peking and concludes with the peace negotiations and withdrawal of the greater part of the allied forces from China, original editions are excessively rare.

THE CRUISE OF THE PEARL WITH AN ACCOUNT OF THE OPERATIONS OF THE NAVAL BRIGADE IN INDIA
9781843428206
Drawn from the unusual diary of a naval Chaplain detailing the exploits of a scratch Naval Brigade, consisting of warship crews fighting on shore, in quelling the Indian Mutiny in 1857-58. Charming, despite the grim nature of much of the material.

THE LAST CRUISE OF THE "MAJESTIC"
George Goodchild from the log book of Petty Officer J.G. Cowie
9781474539166

Interesting personal account of the service of battleship "Majestic" in the Dardanelles arranged by Goodchild from the logbook of Petty Officer J.G. Cowie. "Majestic" was a Majestic-class pre-dreadnought battleship. In early 1915, she was dispatched to the Mediterranean for service in the Dardanelles Campaign. She participated in bombardments of Turkish forts and supported the Allied landings at Gallipoli. On 27 May 1915, she was torpedoed by the German submarine U-21 at Cape Helles, sinking with the loss of 49 men.

THE COMMISSION OF HMS TERRIBLE 1898-1902
9781843425533

Naval Brigades in South African War & China 1900. Various nominal rolls.

THE NAVAL BRIGADE IN SOUTH AFRICA DURING THE YEARS 1877-78-79
9781843429203

An account of the actions of the Naval Brigade from 'HMS Active' in South Africa's Kaffir and Zulu wars in 1877-79. Written by the Brigade's principal medical officer.

THE HISTORY OF THE BALTIC CAMPAIGN OF 1854, FROM DOCUMENTS AND OTHER MATERIALS FURNISHED BY VICE-ADMIRAL SIR C. NAPIER
9781845742126

A full history of the Crimean War's 'forgotten' sideshow in the Baltic, based on the papers of the British Commander, Admiral Napier, which exonerates him from charges of incompetence.

www.ingramcontent.com/pod-product-compliance
Lightning Source LLC
LaVergne TN
LVHW061220060426
835508LV00014B/1372

* 9 7 8 1 4 7 4 5 4 0 9 0 2 *